Contents

Compiled November 2024

Chess

- The longest chess game ever recorded occurred between I. Nikolic and Arsovic in Belgrade in 1989, lasting 269 moves and ending in a draw.
- The term "Checkmate" is derived from the Persian phrase "Shah Mat," meaning "the King is dead."
- The first chess match held in outer space was on June 9, 1970, between space and Earth, concluding in a draw.
- In 1280, Spain introduced the rule allowing pawns to advance two squares on their first move.

- The number of unique possible chess games far exceeds the number of electrons in the universe, estimated at about 10^120.
- The longest theoretical chess game can last up to 5,949 moves.
- The first known chessboard with alternating light and dark squares appeared in Europe in 1090.
- During World War II, some of the best chess players in the world served as codebreakers.
- Garry Kasparov became the youngest world chess champion at the age of 22.
- Alan Turing developed the world's first computer chess program in 1951.
- Chess Rules Overview:
- Chess is played on an eight-by-eight grid of 64 squares with alternating colors. Each player starts with sixteen pieces: one king, one queen, two rooks, two bishops, two knights, and eight pawns. The game aims to checkmate the opponent's king.
- Each piece moves uniquely:
- King: Moves one square in any direction.
- Queen: Moves any number of squares in any direction.
- Rook: Moves any number of squares horizontally or vertically.
- Bishop: Moves any number of squares diagonally.
- Knight: Moves in an 'L' shape. It is the only piece that can leap over others.
- Pawn: Moves one square forward but can move two squares on its first turn. Pawns capture one square diagonally forward.

Strawberries

- Strawberries are the first fruit to ripen in spring.
- Each strawberry has over 200 seeds on its surface.
- Belonging to the rose family, strawberries' botanical name is Fragaria.
- Ancient Romans cultivated strawberries as early as 200 BC.
- California leads U.S. production by shipping 10 million baskets daily during harvest.
- Eight medium strawberries contain approximately 50 calories.

- Strawberries provide ample Vitamin C, potassium, and fiber.
- Belgium hosts a museum dedicated solely to strawberries.
- Unlike other fruits, strawberries have seeds outside.
- Strawberries come in various colors, including red, white, pink, yellow, and golden.
- Botanically, strawberries are not true berries; they are aggregate fruits.
- There are 103 different species of strawberries.
- A phobia related to strawberries is called fragariaphobia.
- Strawberry plants are perennials.
- Strawberries have more vitamin C than oranges.
- On average, Americans consume eight pounds of strawberries yearly.
- California produces about 90% of U.S. strawberries.
- Strawberries block cancer-causing substances and retroviruses.
- Up to 9% of adults and 6-8% of children under three have strawberry allergies.

Diesel

- Diesel engines achieve around 40% efficiency, compared to gasoline engines' 20%.
- Diesel fuel is less flammable than gasoline.
- U.S. biodiesel production increased from around 10 million gallons in 2002 to 969 million gallons in 2012.
- Due to turbochargers, diesel engines perform better than gasoline ones at high altitudes.
- Modern diesel engines meet pollution criteria similar to gasoline engines, thanks to particulate filters.

- Optimal diesel engine performance occurs below 65 miles per hour.
- Diesel vehicles emit fewer carbon dioxide and run efficiently, making them eco-friendly.
- Inventor Rudolf Diesel originally designed his engine to run on peanut oil.
- Diesel engines have higher compression ratios, enhancing efficiency.
- Diesel demonstrated his engine at the 1900 World's Fair in Paris on peanut oil.
- Modern diesel engines are cleaner, quieter, and more efficient.
- Diesel engines power massive ships transporting goods globally.
- Properly maintained diesel engines can endure hundreds of thousands of miles.
- Producing more torque, diesel engines are ideal for heavy-duty vehicles.
- Diesel engines travel further on the same amount of fuel compared to gasoline engines.
- They are used in cars, trucks, buses, boats, and even some aircraft.
- Diesel engines can run on fuels like biodiesel and vegetable oil.
- Often used in backup generators, diesel engines are reliable and efficient.

Number 1

- The number 1 is the first positive natural number.
- It's the sole number neither prime nor composite.
- Known as the multiplicative identity or unit.
- Symbolises unity and singularity.
- In programming, Boolean values use 1 for true and 0 for false.
- Statistically, the number 1 appears more frequently in lists of data.
- Multiplying or dividing any number by one yields that number.

- One can only be divided by itself.
- As an identity element, 8 multiplied by 1 equals 1 multiplied by 8, both equaling 8.
- Terms for unique entities often use "one," like "cyclops" for one-eyed creatures and "dromedary" for camels with one hump.
- In numerology, it represents unity, beginnings, and divinity.
- The Tarot card numbered 1, The Magician, signifies new beginnings and manifestation.
- Hydrogen, the most abundant element, has an atomic number of 1.
- In some faiths, 1 represents universal unity and divine creation.
- The Chinese symbol for 1, a horizontal line, signifies a new journey.

- Historically, number 1 was considered prime. Modern definitions exclude it, because a prime must have two distinct positive divisors.

- When raised to any power, the number 1 remains 1

Perfume

- Perfume smells differently on individuals due to unique skin chemistry.
- Eau de toilette has 10% perfume concentration; eau de parfum has about 15%, while actual Parfum exceeds 20%.
- Best applied after a shower or on hydrated skin to extend scent longevity.
- Apply on pulse points like the neck, wrists, and behind knees for maximized fragrance.
- Avoid rubbing wrists together after applying perfume to preserve top notes.

- Tapputi, from 1200 BC Babylonian Mesopotamia, is considered the first female chemist and perfumer.
- To correct over-application, use alcohol-soaked cotton balls.
- Perfumes consist of top, middle, and base notes.
- Maceration involves soaking objects in solvents like alcohol to extract aromatic compounds.
- Orris butter, the rarest scent, is drawn from iris rhizomes and can cost more than gold.
- Shumukh by Nabeel is the priciest perfume at $1.29 million, featuring a bottle adorned with silver, gold, and gems.
- The highest-quality roses come from Bulgaria's Rose Valley, producing "Liquid Gold" rose oil.
- Mastering perfumery requires at least 20 years and extensive knowledge of chemistry.
- Jasmine flowers produce essential oils used for stress relief and anxiety reduction.
- Agarwood, a key perfume ingredient, faces extinction threats.
- Ambergris, or whale vomit, is another valuable perfume ingredient, costing between $70,000 and $120,000 per kilogram.
- Some Victoria's Secret floral scents effectively repel mosquitoes.
- Marilyn Monroe famously said she slept wearing only "five drops of Chanel No. 5".
- Perfume derives from the Latin "per fumum," meaning "through smoke."

Bread

- Bread has long been known as the "staff of life."
- Historically, bakers made enough bread to last a week given its lengthy baking process.
- Twist tie colors on bread packages indicate the baking day.
- Bread, made from flour and water dough, is one of the oldest artificial foods and remains globally popular.
- Egyptians first added yeast to create lighter bread.
- Humans ate bread at least 14,400 years ago, and it remains a dietary staple.

- Greeks learned bread-making from Egyptians, spreading it across Europe.
- In ancient Rome, bread and wheat were deemed more critical than meat, supporting Roman welfare distributions.
- A person's social class could historically be deduced by bread color; darker bread indicated lower status.
- Toast is sliced bread browned by radiant heat.
- The longest loaf of bread ever made measured 1.2 km.
- The Great Fire of London began in a bakery.
- John Montagu, the 4th Earl of Sandwich, inspired the sandwich's name when he started pairing bread with meat.
- In medieval Europe, bakers often made bread with a cross to ward off evil spirits.
- Traditional bread is banned on the International Space station as the crumbs could cause major issues. Instead, astronauts use tortillas.
- Ancient brewers used old bread as a starter to brew beer.
- Hardtack, a type pf long-lasting dry bread, was a staple for soldiers in wars because it could be stored for months without spoiling.

Plastic

- Leo Baekeland created the first synthetic plastic in 1907.
- Each year, more than 300 million tons of plastic are manufactured globally.
- Only about 9% of all plastic ever made has been recycled.
- Plastics can take up to 1,000 years to break down in landfills.
- Parkesine, the first plant-based plastic, appeared in 1862.
- In 1957, Disneyland showcased a "Plastics Home of the Future" built almost entirely from plastic.

- Cellophane, one of the earliest transparent plastics, was invented in 1908.
- Bakelite, called the "Material of a Thousand Uses," was utilized in many products including telephones and cameras.
- Alphabet
- Today's alphabet traces back to the Latin script used by Romans.
- The English alphabet has 26 letters.
- "A" has been used since ancient times as the first alphabet letter.
- "E" is the most frequently used letter in English.
- "Z" is the least commonly used.
- The alphabet evolved, adding or removing letters through time.
- The dot above the letter "i" is called a tittle.
- Once considered the 27th letter, the ampersand (&) has a rich history.
- Critical for literacy, the alphabet facilitates written communication.
- "Alphabet" combines "alpha" and "beta" from the Greek lettering system.
- The 26 English letters represent over 40 distinct sounds.
- Roughly 100 languages use the same alphabet as English.
- The longest English word without an "E" is "floccinaucinihilipilification."
- A pangram, a sentence with all 26 letters, includes: "The quick brown fox jumps over the lazy dog."

Coffee

- Coffee was first chewed by African tribes who combined ground beans with animal fat for energy balls.
- Decaffeinated coffee supplies caffeine to soda and pharmaceutical industries.
- Instant coffee has been around since 1771.
- The average American spends around $2000 annually on coffee.
- Finland leads global coffee consumption with an average of four cups daily per person.

- Beethoven required exactly 60 beans for each cup of coffee he consumed.
- Brazilian athletes funded their 1932 Olympic journey by selling coffee en-route to Los Angeles.
- Historical attempts to ban coffee cited its capacity to stimulate radical thought.
- The Guiness record holder for the oldest cat drank coffee daily.
- In 1674, British women's opposition branded coffee as harmful.
- Ethiopian farmers' goats, dancing after eating Coffea plants, spurred the legend of coffee.
- Arabica and Robusta are the two types of coffee beans, with Arabica being the more popular.
- Coffee beans are pits from berries that resemble legumes.
- Hawaii and California grow coffee within the United States.
- Brazil leads global coffee production, doubling Vietnam's output.
- Coffee cherries are eaten directly, and early enthusiasts mixed them with fat for energy balls.
- Kopi Luwak, derived from civet faeces, is the world's most expensive coffee.
- Finland consumes the most coffee per capita, averaging 27.5 pounds yearly.
- In Italian, "espresso" means "pressed out."
- Coffee is the second most valuable traded commodity after petroleum.

Books

- The longest book ever written exceeds a million words.
- The first printed book originated in China.
- The tiniest book in the world measures merely 0.07 mm by 0.10 mm.
- Some books are encased in human skin.
- There is a book that requires heating to be read.
- J.K. Rowling experienced rejection from 12 publishers before Harry Potter was accepted.
- The term 'bookworm' originally referred to an insect that consumes books.

- The distinct aroma of old books is termed "bibliosmia".
- Reading can help lower stress levels.
- President Theodore Roosevelt had the habit of reading a book daily.
- The Tale of Genji is often considered the first novel written.
- Books were once chained to shelves during the Middle Ages.
- Iceland boasts the highest per capita rates of writers, book publications, and reading.
- A completely wordless book exists.
- The Bible holds the title for the most stolen book worldwide.
- The Bible is also the most translated book.
- Amazon's first book sold was a science textbook.
- An entire novel has been written without the use of the letter 'e'.

Laptops

- Laptops were initially called "portable computers," but it was evident that no one actually carried them around.
- Surprisingly, the most frequently used key on a laptop is not the "Enter" key, but the "Delete" key.
- In 1981, Adam Osborne invented the first laptop, named the Osborne 1. This machine weighed 24.5 pounds and featured a 5-inch screen.
- The term "laptop" was introduced in 1983. The first laptop with a color display was the Commodore SX-64, released in 1984.

- The Acer Swift 7 holds the title for the world's thinnest laptop at just 9.98 mm thick.
- The priciest laptop ever sold is the Luvaglio One Million Dollar Laptop, which costs $1 million.
- Released in 1982, the Grid Compass 1101 was the first laptop with a touchscreen.
- On average, a laptop contains around 1,000 parts.
- The Apple iSight, launched in 2003, was the first laptop with a built-in webcam.
- The MacBook Air, released in 2008, was the pioneer for laptops with a solid-state drive (SSD).
- The IBM ThinkPad T42, introduced in 2004, was the first laptop with a fingerprint scanner.
- Apple's PowerBook G4, launched in 2001, had the first backlit keyboard.
- The Toshiba Satellite 1955, released in 2002, was the initial laptop with a built-in DVD drive.
- The Apple iBook, released in 1999, was the first laptop to feature a built-in Wi-Fi card.
- The IBM ThinkPad T30, unveiled in 2002, contained the first built-in Bluetooth card.
- Lastly, the Panasonic Toughbook CF-18, launched in 2003, was the first laptop equipped with a built-in GPS card.

Soap

- The word "soap" originates from the Latin term "sapo," which means soap or a type of clay.
- The earliest evidence of soap-like substances dates back to approximately 2800 BC in Ancient Babylon.
- Babylonians discovered how to create soap by boiling fats with ashes and water.
- In ancient times, soap was predominantly used in the textile industry to clean and prepare fabrics for further treatment.

- Ancient Egyptians, Greeks, and Romans made soap by combining fat, oils, and salts.
- In Egypt, the notable Ebers Papyrus from 1500 BC references the use of soap-like materials for personal hygiene and medicinal purposes.
- By the 12th century, soap-making began to flourish in England, with the Celts being among the first to produce soap using animal fat and plant ashes. Soap-making became a major industry in Europe during the Middle Ages.
- In the 18th century, the British company Pears began producing transparent soap, which remains popular today.
- The world's most expensive soap, costing around $2,700 for a 160-gram piece, is made in Qatar and includes diamond and gold powder.
- During the Middle Ages, soap was as valuable as gold, making it unaffordable for most people.
- The expression "soap my neck" is present in both Russian and Japanese, having different meanings in each language.
- Although solid soap was first made thousands of years ago, it was extremely costly and only accessible to nobility.
- Soap prices dropped significantly in the 1930s due to the invention of an inexpensive and rapid production method in the USA and Europe.
- In 1880, Procter & Gamble introduced a new brand of white soap that gained popularity because it floated in water.

Glasses

- Glasses were invented in 1000 A.D. The Romans discovered that glass had properties useful for reading small texts, leading to the invention of the magnifying glass, also known as a "reading stone".
- The first wearable glasses appeared in Italy in the 13th century. Renaissance paintings depict scholars using perch-style glasses or handheld frames.
- During the Renaissance, glasses were a symbol of intelligence. Scholars with eyesight problems were often

- seen wearing glasses, associating them with intelligence, wealth, and property.
- The 'Martin's Margins' are named after Benjamin Martin, an instrument maker in London, who is considered one of the first inventors of modern glasses.
- Benjamin Franklin invented the bifocal lens, allowing individuals with both myopia and hyperopia to see using one pair of glasses.
- Sunglasses were invented in the 12th century by the Chinese to obscure judges' eyes in court.
- The first frames were made of wood, copper, leather, and bone.
- Spanish inventors attached ribbons to glasses to keep them from slipping down the nose.
- The modern style of glasses that rest on the bridge of the nose was created in the 18th century.
- Some people believe that wearing gold earrings and glasses at the same time can improve vision, although this is likely a myth.
- Reading in dim light won't damage your sight, although good light makes reading easier.
- Most glasses are now made of plastic, not glass.
- About 25% of the world population wears prescription glasses or corrective lenses.
- Famous singer Elton John has an impressive collection of glasses.
- The oldest glasses in the world date back to the 13th century.
- The most expensive glasses in the world are made by Chopard and cost $400,000.
- John Lennon wore his round-rimmed glasses to correct his nearsightedness.
- Ray-Ban aviators were originally designed for pilots in the 1930s.

Umbrellas

- The word "umbrella" originates from the Latin term "umbra," which means shade or shadow.
- The earliest recorded use of umbrellas dates back to ancient Egypt around 3,000 BC.
- The Chinese were pioneers in creating a collapsible fabric dome around 21 CE.
- In ancient societies, umbrellas often symbolized authority and high status.

- Traditional umbrellas were crafted from luxurious materials such as silk, whereas modern ones utilize materials like nylon or polyester.
- The oldest existing umbrella, over 2,000 years old, was unearthed in China.
- The largest umbrella in the world, called the "Umbrella of the Sun," is located in Las Palmas, Gran Canaria, with a diameter of 28 meters.
- Historically, umbrellas were predominantly used by women and regarded as symbols of femininity.
- The 19th century brought major advancements in umbrella design, including the introduction of buttons for automatic opening and closing.
- The U.S. Patent Office has been flooded with various designs aimed at improving umbrellas, showcasing relentless innovation.
- Certain cultures celebrate umbrellas through festivals dedicated to their craftsmanship.
- In Victorian England, there were distinct etiquette rules concerning the carrying and usage of umbrellas.
- There are museums devoted to umbrellas, exhibiting their rich history and development.

Printers

- Charles Babbage invented the first mechanical printer in the 19th century.
- Laser printers use a laser beam on a drum to transfer images to paper.
- 3D printers build objects from digital files using materials like plastic and metal.
- Printer ink is more expensive per gallon than fine champagne.
- Laser printers consume more energy than desktop computers while printing.

- The PrintStik, measuring 2 x 2 x 11 inches, is the world's smallest printer.
- Big Image Systems' Infinitus printer can print up to 2,000 square feet.
- The fastest printers produce up to 150 pages per minute.
- One year's worth of empty ink cartridges would circle the earth three times if placed end-to-end.
- Johannes Gutenberg's printing press dates back to the 15th century.
- PrinCube, the smallest mobile color printer, fits in your pocket and prints on various surfaces.
- The HP Deskjet 3755 is the smallest all-in-one printer.
- Laser printer fuser rollers can reach nearly 400°F.
- Some 3D printers can construct entire houses using concrete.
- Producing one printer cartridge uses about a gallon of oil factoring manufacturing and transportation.
- NASA has used 3D printers aboard the International Space Station for making tools and parts.

Scissors

- The earliest known scissors appeared in ancient Egypt around 1500 BCE.
- The Romans are credited with the cross-bladed design. Robert Hinchliffe, an Englishman, received the first scissors patent in 1761.
- Sheffield, England, became renowned for quality scissors in the 18th century.
- Surgeons hold their scissors with thumb and ring finger for stability.
- In the Middle Ages, scissors were luxury items, often decorated with precious materials.
- Most scissors cater to right-handers, but left-handed versions are now common.
- In China, it's believed pregnant women shouldn't hold scissors near the marital bed to prevent birth defects.
- High-end scissors like Sasuke Bonsai Scissors can cost up to $35,000 due to their craftsmanship.
- Scissors are frequently left inside patients after surgery.
- They require professional sharpening and oiling at the pivot for optimal function.
- Contemporary artists like Henri Matisse used scissors to create intricate paper cut-outs, a technique he called "drawing with scissors".
- The first pivoted scissors appeared in Mesopotamia around 100 AD.
- In Victorian times, scissors were often worn as part of a chatelaine (a chain belt) for easy access.

Socks

- The oldest known socks, from 300-500 AD Egypt, were designed for sandals.
- Early socks were likely toe socks.
- By the 8th century, Greeks used matted animal fur for socks.
- William Lee's 1589 knitting machine was made for knitting socks.
- Before trousers, men wore knee-high socks or stockings.
- Wealthy individuals once showcased status with silk socks.
- Lost socks often end up in washing machine drums or corners.
- Datang, China, is the "Sock Capital of the World," producing billions annually.
- "National Sock Day" on December 4th celebrates fun sock-themed holidays.
- In some cultures, showing socks in formal settings is inappropriate.
- The largest sock ever, over 60 feet long, was made in 2011.
- Compression socks help blood circulation and are popular among athletes and travellers.

Calculators

- The abacus, invented around 2500 BC in Sumeria, is the earliest known calculating tool.
- John Napier created a rod-based multiplication and division tool in 1617.
- Wilhelm Schickard made the first adding machine in 1623, followed by Blaise Pascal's mechanical calculator, the Pascaline, in 1643.
- The Arithmometer, developed in 1820, was the first commercially produced mechanical calculator.
- IBM launched the first all-transistor calculator in 1954, reducing size and power consumption.
- Texas Instruments released the handheld TI-2500 Datamath in 1967.
- Specialized calculators are used for financial calculations and graphing calculators aid in education.
- Vintage models like the HP-35 are now valuable collector's items.

SHAMPOO

Shampoo

- Shampoo originated in India using herbs and berries.
- Hans Schwarzkopf introduced the first commercial shampoo in Germany in 1903.
- Before that, people used soap bars, which left residue.
- Head & Shoulders, an anti-dandruff shampoo, debuted in 1961.
- Dry shampoo has been around since the 1940s.
- Purple shampoo neutralizes brassy tones in blonde hair.
- Eco-friendly solid shampoo bars are also available.
- The global shampoo market was worth about $31.32 billion in 2021, with major brands like P&G's Aussie, Unilever's Dove, and Alberto VO5.
- Shampoos are made with surfactants such as sodium lauryl sulfate.
- Different cultures have unique hair-washing practices, like using clay powder in Asia during the late 15th century.

Candles

- The oldest recorded candles were found in China, dating to 200 BC.
- Ancient Egyptians used beeswax candles for rituals around 3000 BC.
- Romans first added fragrances like cinnamon and lavender to candles.
- Tallow was commonly used for candles in the Middle Ages.
- Beeswax candles were a luxury then due to their sweet scent and clean burn.
- The longest burning candle lasted 30 days, and the tallest one stood at 153 feet, lit in China in 2015.
- Early wicks were hemp before cotton became common.
- Candlemaking, or chandlery, has been practiced for centuries and continues today with modern methods.

Paperclips

- Before the advent of paperclips, ribbons were used as early as the 13th century to bind papers together.
- Samuel B. Fay received the first patent for a clip-like device in 1867, originally intended for attaching tickets to fabric.
- The Gem paperclip, now the most ubiquitous design, was never patented.
- During World War II, Norwegians symbolically wore paperclips to show their resistance and unity against the Nazi occupation.
- Operation Paperclip was a covert U.S. initiative to enlist German scientists post-World War II.
- Kyle MacDonald famously bartered his way from a red paperclip to a house through a series of online trades.
- Steel paperclips, being magnetic, are often employed in various science experiments.
- Depending on its size and material, a single paperclip can secure up to 20 sheets of paper.

Clocks

- In 1656, Christiaan Huygens developed the pendulum clock, improving daily accuracy from 15 minutes to 15 seconds.
- A Colorado institute created an exceptionally precise clock that will neither lose nor gain a second in 20 million years.
- Two scientists validated time dilation by flying with atomic clocks around the globe; these clocks indicated different times upon their return.

- Artist Siren Elise Wilhelmsen designed a clock that knits a scarf annually.
- The term "o'clock" is a contraction of "stroke of the clock" from medieval mechanical clocks.
- When the second hand appears stationary, it is due to your brain extending your perception of time.
- France used a decimal clock that divided the day into 10 hours.
- Before the advent of alarm clocks, knocker-uppers would wake people by knocking on their doors. At sea level, a pendulum clock loses about 16 seconds each day at an altitude of 4000 feet.
- Drawing a clock face serves as a screening test for Alzheimer's and other forms of dementia.
- A second is officially defined by 9,192,631,770 oscillations of a Cesium atom.
- In 2007, a group clandestinely repaired the antique clock in the French Pantheon, which led to legal issues.
- Clocks occasionally strike 23:59:60 to synchronize with Earth's rotation, resulting in a 61-second minute.
- The railroad industry standardized train schedules by implementing time zones in 1883.
- Built in 1386, the Salisbury Cathedral Clock is recognized as the oldest working clock worldwide.
- Peter Henlein introduced the pocket watch in 1504, making portable timekeeping possible.
- GMT (Greenwich Mean Time) was established in 1675 at the Royal Observatory in Greenwich, London.
- John Harrison's marine chronometer revolutionized 18th-century navigation with its precise timekeeping capabilities at sea.
- In 1840, Alexander Bain created the first electric clock, powered by an electrochemical battery.

Mirrors

- Early mirrors were made from polished stone like obsidian around 6000 BC.
- Polished copper mirrors emerged in Mesopotamia around 4000 BC.
- In 1835, German chemist Justus von Liebig invented modern mirrors with a silver-coated glass layer.
- Breaking a mirror being unlucky for seven years comes from Roman times.
- Leonardo da Vinci used mirror writing for many of his notes, readable only through reflection.
- Venice's 16th-century mirrors were costly and prized.
- Infinity Mirrors create endless light tunnels using two parallel mirrors.
- The Mirror Test checks animal self-awareness through mirror recognition.
- Periscopes use mirrors to see over obstacles, while reflecting telescopes gather distant light with mirrors.
- Invented in 1911, rearview mirrors are crucial for safe driving.
- Mirror images reverse left and right, making text appear backward.
- Modern mirrors often use aluminium or silver for better reflectivity.
- Smart mirrors display information such as the weather, news, and time.
- The Hubble Space Telescope captures space images with a large mirror.

Headphones

- Nathaniel Baldwin invented the first headphones in 1910, crafting them by hand in his kitchen and selling them to the U.S. Navy.
- The introduction of stereo sound in the 1950s paved the way for the creation of stereo headphones aimed at music lovers.
- Pilots were the initial beneficiaries of noise-cancelling headphones, which were engineered to reduce engine noise during flights.
- Bone conduction headphones work by transmitting sound through the bones of the skull directly to the inner ear, bypassing the eardrums.
- Dallyn Rule, a Canadian artist, created the largest headphones ever for Mini Maker Faire in Vancouver.
- Wireless headphones first appeared in the 1960s, utilizing radio waves to transmit audio signals.
- The Sony Walkman, released in 1979, significantly increased the popularity of headphones among the general public.
- Headphones with Planar Magnetic Technology offer precise sound reproduction and minimize certain distortions.
- Extended use of headphones at high volumes can cause hearing damage, highlighting the need for safe listening habits.

Remote controls

- The Zenith Radio Corporation developed the first TV remote control, "Lazy Bones," in 1950.
- Connected by a wire, it was followed by Eugene Polley's wireless "Flashmatic" in 1955, which used light.
- In 1956, Robert Adler created the "Space Command" remote with ultrasonic sound.
- Steve Wozniak designed the first universal remote in the 1980s. Nowadays, most remotes use infrared light.
- The largest TV remote, made by two Indian brothers, spans over 14 feet.
- Nikola Tesla showcased an early remote in 1898 by controlling a toy boat with radio waves.
- The first toy car with remote control was released in the 1960s.
- NASA employs remote controls for Mars rovers.
- During WWII, German and American forces used remote-controlled bombs and torpedoes.
- Some advanced toilets now feature remotes to adjust water pressure and seat temperature.

Cameras

- The concept of the camera has its roots in ancient China and Greece with the invention of the camera obscura, a device that projected images of its surroundings onto a screen.
- Joseph Nicéphore Niépce captured the first photograph ever taken in 1826 or 1827, titled "View from the Window at Le Gras".
- Louis Daguerre's invention of the daguerreotype in 1839 marked the first commercially successful photographic process.

- James Clerk Maxwell shot the first color photograph in 1861 using three different color filters.
- Steven Sasson at Kodak developed the first digital camera in 1975. It weighed around 8 pounds and took 23 seconds to capture one image.
- The oldest existing photograph, taken by Joseph Nicéphore Niépce, is nearly 200 years old.
- Gaspard-Félix Tournachon, also known as Nadar, took the first aerial photograph over Paris in 1858.
- Charles Martin captured the first underwater photograph in the Bahamas in 1925.
- Louis Daguerre unexpectedly took the first photograph of a person in 1838 while capturing a street scene.
- Robert Cornelius took the first selfie in 1839.
- Julius Berkowski photographed the first solar eclipse in 1851.
- The Polaroid Model 95, released in 1948, was the first instant camera, allowing users to see their photos immediately.
- The Hasselblad camera used during the Apollo 11 mission in 1969 captured the first photographs on the Moon.
- The Voigtländer Zoomar, introduced in 1959, was the first camera with a zoom lens.
- Canon EOS-1N RS, introduced in 1995, was the first camera featuring image stabilization technology.
- Fujifilm FinePix S3 Pro, launched in 2004, was the first camera with face detection technology.
- Nikon Coolpix P1, introduced in 2005, was the first camera with built-in Wi-Fi.
- The most viewed photograph in history is "Bliss," the default wallpaper for Windows XP, taken by Charles O'Rear.

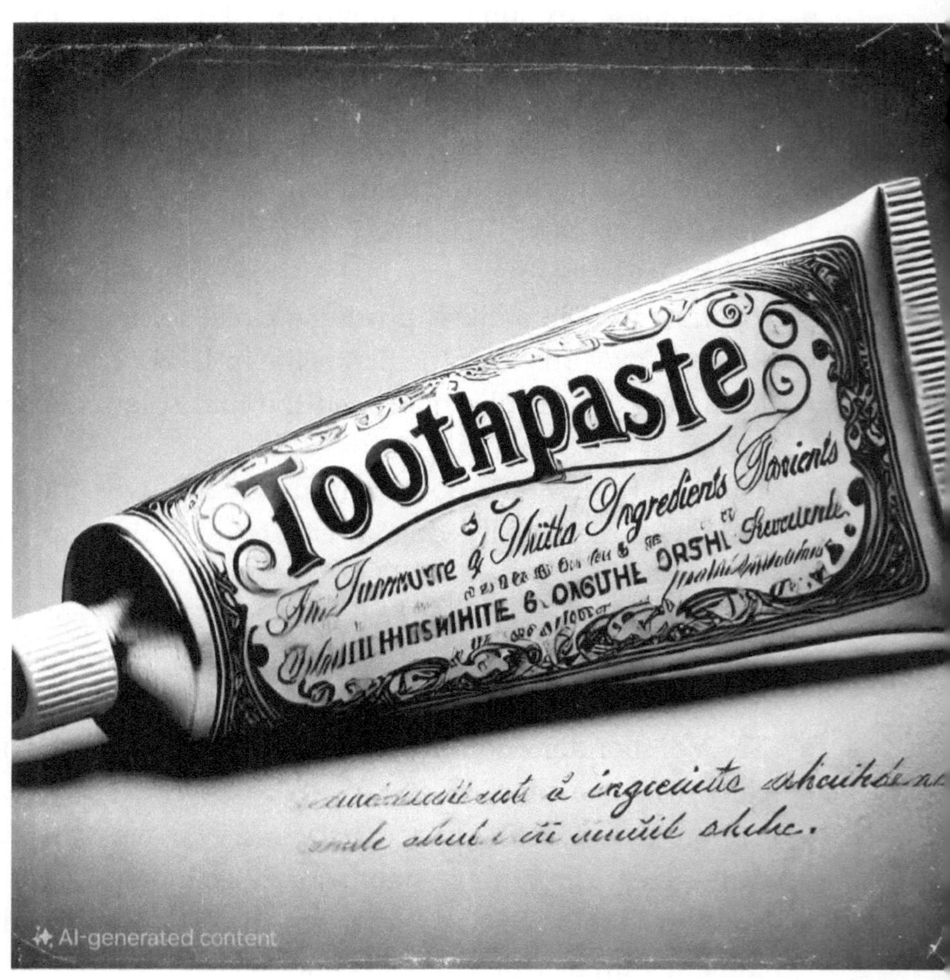
Toothpaste

AI-generated content

Toothpaste

- The first toothpaste was made around 5000 BC in ancient Egypt from ox hooves' ashes, myrrh, burnt eggshells, and pumice.
- Greeks and Romans used crushed bones and oyster shells, while the Chinese and Indians used herbal mints, ginseng, and salt around 500 BC.
- Colgate started mass-producing toothpaste in jars in 1873, and Dr. Washington Sheffield introduced collapsible tubes in 1892.
- Fluoride was added in 1914 to prevent cavities.
- Modern toothpaste includes fluoride, abrasives like hydrated aluminum oxides and baking soda, flavors, humectants, and detergents.
- Ingredients such as glycerol prevent drying out, and some contain hydrogen peroxide for stain removal or potassium nitrate for sensitivity.
- Toothpaste expires two years after manufacture and is a non-Newtonian fluid.
- In South Korea, red ginseng toothpaste is valued for its health benefits.

Playing cards

- Playing cards are believed to have originated in China during the Tang Dynasty in the 9th century.
- A standard deck's 52 cards symbolize the 52 weeks in a year, with the four suits representing the four seasons.
- The face cards (King, Queen, Jack) are thought to depict historical figures; for instance, the King of Hearts is often linked to Charlemagne.
- The Joker card was invented in the United States during the 19th century specifically for the game Euchre.

- During World War II, soldiers painted the Ace of Spades on their helmets for good fortune.
- The number of possible permutations of a 52-card deck is an astronomical 52^52, a figure with 68 digits.
- In early Chinese card games, players used cards made from ivory, wood, and other materials before paper became widespread.
- Originally, court cards (King, Queen, Jack) were termed King, Knight, and Knave.
- The red and black colors in a deck are believed to symbolize day and night.
- Interesting facts about shuffling include that performing eight perfect faro shuffles will restore a deck to its original order.
- The four suits are thought to represent the classes of medieval society: hearts (clergy), spades (nobility), diamonds (merchants), and clubs (peasants).
- The first printed playing cards appeared in Europe in the 14th century.
- The record for the tallest house of cards stands over 25 feet tall, constructed from more than 2,500 decks.
- Finally, it wasn't until the 15th century that female characters began appearing in playing cards.

Razors

- The earliest razors were made from materials like flint, shark teeth, and clam shells, dating back to prehistoric times.
- Ancient Egyptians used razors made from copper and solid gold, as discovered in tombs from the 4th millennium BC.
- Romans used iron razors and were among the first to popularize daily shaving.
- The first safety razor was designed by King Camp Gillette in 1901, revolutionizing personal grooming.
- Also known as cut-throat razors, these were the primary shaving tool before the invention of safety razors.
- The first electric razor was patented by Jacob Schick in 1928.
- Introduced in the 1960s, disposable razors provided a convenient and affordable shaving option.
- In the 16th century, King Henry VIII of England imposed a tax on beards, which increased with the beard wearer's social status.
- Alexander the Great required his soldiers to shave to prevent enemies from grabbing their beards in battle.
- Contrary to popular belief, shaving does not cause hair to grow back thicker or faster.
- The average man will shave more than 20,000 times in his lifetime.
- Pogonophobia is the fear of beards.

Shoes

- Sneakers earned their name because they were so q
- uiet, you could "sneak" around in them.
- Originally, high heels were designed for men, especially for horse riding.
- The oldest known shoes are sagebrush bark sandals, dating back to around 7,000-8,000 BC.
- Celine Dion has a collection of over 3,000 pairs of shoes.
- The most expensive shoes ever sold are the ruby slippers from "The Wizard of Oz," which fetched $660,000.

- Modern shoelaces were invented by Harvey Kennedy in 1790.
- Platform shoes were popular in ancient Venice to keep wearers above mud and sludge.
- Boots with elastic sides were popularized by Queen Victoria in the 1830s.
- The first standardized shoe size was based on barleycorns.
- Neil Armstrong's moon boots remain on the moon.
- Robert Wadlow, the tallest man ever, wore size 37AA shoes.
- Christian Louboutin's iconic red soles were inspired by an assistant's red nail polish.
- Flip-flops date back approximately 4,000 years to ancient Egypt.
- In China, lotus shoes were used for foot binding, a practice that restricted proper walking.
- Shoes in dreams can symbolize being grounded or resourceful.
- Wedges were created during World War II due to material shortages.
- Shoe addiction, also known as altocalciphilia, is a real phenomenon.
- King Tutankhamun's tomb contained ornate flip-flops.
- Shoes designed specifically for left and right feet didn't appear until the 1800s.
- Astronauts' boots are constructed to endure the harsh conditions of space.
- Ancient Greeks often went barefoot, considering shoes unnecessary.
- Roman soldiers wore sandals, and more laces indicated higher rank.

Dice

- Dice have a history that stretches back over 5,000 years, with some of the earliest examples discovered in Mesopotamia.
- Initially, dice were crafted from the knucklebones of animals.
- In ancient Egypt, dice were a part of games like Senet, which dates back to 3000 BCE.
- The Romans, known for their enthusiasm for gambling, used dice made from materials such as bone, ivory, and metal.
- Beyond the traditional six-sided dice, there are various other shapes, including 4, 8, 10, 12, and 20-sided dice.
- On a standard six-sided die, the numbers on the opposite faces always total seven.
- Kevin Cook holds the world's largest collection of dice, boasting more than 50,000 pieces.
- Dice are also mentioned in ancient literature, such as the Indian Rigveda and the Bible.

Erasers

- Before the use of rubber, breadcrumbs were utilized for erasing pencil marks.
- Joseph Priestley, known for discovering oxygen, also found that rubber could erase pencil marks.
- British engineer Edward Nairne sold the first rubber erasers in the 1770s.
- In 1858, Hymen Lipman received the first patent for attaching an eraser to a pencil.
- In the UK, erasers are often referred to as "rubbers".
- The classic pink eraser is composed of synthetic rubber and pumice.
- Vulcanization, discovered by Charles Goodyear, enhanced the durability of rubber erasers.
- It's a misconception that erasers can fully remove ink; most ink erasers work by removing the top layer of the paper.

GLUE

Glue

- Early humans used natural adhesives like plant resins and animal glues around 200,000 years ago.
- Neanderthals employed tar-like substances for attaching tools and weapons.
- Ancient Egyptians used collagen-based glues in mummification and furniture-making.
- "Ward's paste," the first synthetic adhesive, was invented by British scientist Joshua Ward in 1750.
- Accidentally discovered in 1942 by Dr. Harry Coover, Super Glue was first dismissed for its excessive stickiness.
- Introduced in 1955, PVA glue is known for its versatility and ease of use.
- The Penny Black, issued in 1840 UK, was the first adhesive postage stamp.
- Henkel AG & Co. KGaA, founded in 1876, is a leading global adhesive maker.
- A 201.4-meter wooden bridge in China set a record in 2019 using 71,460 liters of glue.
- Nanogate used just 0.6 milligrams of adhesive in 2011, setting a Guinness World Record.
- Traditional animal collagen glues, like hide glue, remain in use for certain applications.

Light bulbs

- The first electric light was made in 1800 by Humphry Davy.
- Thomas Edison and Joseph Swan independently developed the first practical incandescent bulbs in the 1870s.
- Early light bulbs used carbon filaments before tungsten became the standard.
- The Centennial Light in California has been burning since 1901 and is still glowing.
- Incandescent bulbs convert only about 10% of the energy they use into light; the rest is heat.
- LED bulbs can last up to 50,000 hours, significantly longer than incandescent bulbs.
- The first visible LED was invented by Nick Holonyak in 1962.
- Incandescent bulbs have a perfect Color Rendering Index (CRI) of 100, meaning they render colors most accurately.
- The standard base for light bulbs, known as the Edison Screw, was developed by Thomas Edison.
- CFL bulbs contain a small amount of mercury, which requires careful disposal.
- The first patent for an electric light bulb was filed by Frederick de Moleyns in 1841.
- Lumens measure the brightness of a bulb, while watts measure energy consumption.

Gloves

- Gloves have been worn since ancient times, with evidence of their use in Egypt, Greece, and Rome.
- Linen gloves were found in King Tutankhamun's tomb, dating back to the 14th century B.C.
- Leather boxing gloves from around 120 A.D. were discovered in a Roman fort in England.
- In the Middle Ages, workers like blacksmiths and masons wore gloves for protection.

- Fashion Statement: Gloves became a fashion accessory for women in 16th century Europe, popularized by Queen Catherine de Medici of France.
- English gentlemen used to send gloves to their intended brides as a symbol of their love.
- In the court of King Louis XV of France, gloves were often perfumed.
- In 1834, Xavier Jouvin invented a cutting die that allowed for perfectly fitting gloves.
- During Victorian times, women wore different gloves for various activities, and not wearing gloves was a social faux pas.
- Neil Armstrong's gloves from the Apollo 11 mission still contain lunar dust.
- Quality Control: The FDA uses the Acceptable Quality Level (AQL) to specify the pinhole rate in surgical and examination gloves.
- Glove size is determined by measuring the circumference of the hand around the palm.
- Rubber Gloves were invented in 1894 by William Stewart Halsted to protect medical staff from dermatitis.
- Latex gloves can cause allergic reactions, leading to the use of alternatives like nitrile and vinyl.
- Fingerprints can be lifted from gloves left at crime scenes.

Batteries

- The earliest known batteries, called the Baghdad Batteries, date back to around 200 BC and were used for electroplating.
- Alessandro Volta invented the first true battery, the Voltaic Pile, in 1800.
- A typical battery consists of three main parts: an anode, a cathode, and an electrolyte.
- The first rechargeable battery was the lead-acid battery, invented by Gaston Planté in 1859.
- Lithium-Ion Batteries, widely used in electronics, were commercialized by Sony in 1991.
- Nickel-cadmium batteries suffer from a "memory effect," where they lose capacity if not fully discharged before recharging.
- Batteries can contain harmful chemicals like lead, mercury, and cadmium, which can pollute the environment if not disposed of properly.
- Innovations like graphene batteries and bio-batteries are being explored for their potential to revolutionize energy storage.

Bananas

- The scientific name for banana is Musa sapientum, which means "fruit of the wise men".
- Bananas can float in water because they are less dense than water.
- The banana plant is actually an herb, not a tree.
- Botanically, bananas are classified as berries.
- Around 100 billion bananas are consumed worldwide each year.
- Bananas contain tryptophan, which helps produce serotonin, a mood-enhancing neurotransmitter.
- Bananas originated in Southeast Asia around 8000 BC and are believed to be one of the world's first cultivated fruits.
- India is the largest producer of bananas, followed by China.
- People allergic to latex often have a banana allergy due to similar proteins in both.
- The banana split was invented by David Strickler in 1904 in Latrobe, Pennsylvania.
- The largest bunch of bananas ever recorded contained 473 bananas and weighed 287 pounds.
- Bananas are famously slippery due to polysaccharide molecules in their peels.
- Humans share about 50% of their DNA with bananas.
- Monkeys peel bananas from the bottom up, which is actually easier and less damaging to the fruit.
- There are over 1,000 varieties of bananas, but the Cavendish is the most common.
- The Cavendish banana is under threat from Panama disease, a fungal infection.

Glass

- Glassmaking dates back over 3,500 years to ancient Mesopotamia and Egypt.
- Glass is an amorphous solid, meaning its atoms are not arranged in a regular, repeating pattern.
- Glass is primarily made from silica (silicon dioxide), which is found in sand.
- Glass can occur naturally, such as obsidian from volcanic activity, and can also be man-made.
- Lightning can create a type of natural glass called fulgurite when it strikes sand.

- Unlike crystalline materials, glass does not have a fixed melting point but softens over a range of temperatures.
- Glass can be recycled indefinitely without losing quality or purity.
- Hydrofluoric Acid can dissolve glass, which is used in processes like glass etching.
- Benjamin Franklin invented the glass harmonica in 1761, an instrument made of spinning glass bowls.
- Used for over 1,500 years, stained glass has been a significant art form in religious and secular buildings.
- The Portland Vase, one of the most valuable glass art pieces, is a Roman cameo glass vase dates back to the 1st century AD.
- Most common glass, like windows, is annealed, making it durable but dangerous when broken.
- Tempered Glass: This safety glass shatters into small, less dangerous pieces and is used in car windows and shower doors.
- Glass is an excellent insulator, preventing the passage of heat and electricity.
- Glass does not decompose, emphasizing the importance of recycling.

Paper

- Paper was invented in China around 105 AD by Cai Lun during the Han Dynasty.
- Before paper, ancient Egyptians used papyrus, made from the pith of the papyrus plant.
- The first paper mill in Europe was established in Spain in 1150.
- can be recycled up to seven times before the fibers become too short for further recycling.
- It takes about 5 liters of water to produce a single sheet of paper.
- The Chinese were the first to use paper currency during the Tang Dynasty (618–907 AD).
- The first monthly newspaper, "Notizie Scritte," was printed in Venice in 1556.
- Paper and Methane: Decomposing paper in landfills releases methane, a potent greenhouse gas[3].
- Origami, the art of paper folding, originated in Japan and has been practiced for over a thousand years.
- The Diamond Sutra, printed in China in 868 AD, is the oldest known printed book.

Random

- Flamingos bend their legs at the ankle rather than the knee. Their knees are situated closer to their bodies and hidden by feathers.
- Roller coasters were created to divert Americans from sin. In the 1880s, LaMarcus Thompson built the first roller coaster to offer a fun alternative to saloons and brothels.
- Ice pops were accidentally invented by an 11-year-old. Frank Epperson left soda powder and water outside overnight, and it froze, resulting in the first Popsicle.

- Sloths can hold their breath longer than dolphins. By slowing their heart rates, sloths can remain underwater for up to 40 minutes.
- A woman was elected to Congress before women had the right to vote. Jeanette Rankin was elected in 1916, four years before women's suffrage in the U.S.
- Froot Loops all have the same flavour despite their different colours.
- Supermarket apples can be as old as a year. They are picked, waxed, and stored in cold storage for months before reaching retail shelves.
- It's impossible to hum while holding your nose because air can't escape through your nostrils.
- Octopuses possess three hearts; two circulate blood to the gills, and one supplies the rest of the body.
- Most wasabi paste is not made from real wasabi but rather from horseradish dyed green due to the high cost of genuine wasabi.
- People used to say "prunes" instead of "cheese" when having photographs taken to maintain a more serious expression.
- In the Philippines, McDonald's offers spaghetti served with beef tomato sauce and fried chicken.
- Dunce caps were originally symbols of intelligence. In the 13th century, they were thought to facilitate knowledge transfer to the brain.
- Adolf Hitler was once nominated for a Nobel Peace Prize, although it was ironic, and the nomination was later retracted.
- Lobsters taste with tiny bristles inside their pincers that function as taste buds.
- The British royal family adopted the name Windsor in 1917, changing it from Saxe-Coburg-Gotha to sound less German.
- The Empire State Building has its own ZIP code: 10118.

- The shortest war in history lasted for 38 minutes during the Anglo-Zanzibar War of 1896 when the Sultan fled.
- Blue whale tongues can weigh as much as an elephant, and their hearts can weigh almost a ton.
- The world's largest waterfall is underwater in the Denmark Strait between Greenland and Iceland.
- Michelangelo disliked painting the Sistine Chapel and wrote a poem about his discomfort while doing the work.
- Queen Elizabeth II had a stand-in named Ella Slack for rehearsals to ensure that the sun wouldn't be in her eyes.
- Shadows on the Moon appear darker without an atmosphere to scatter light.
- Some sea cucumbers defend themselves by expelling their internal organs.
- The inventor of the Internet, Tim Berners-Lee, regrets the "https://" format.
- The Statue of Liberty functioned as a lighthouse for 16 years after its dedication.
- The U.S. treasury once produced $100,000 bills for Federal Reserve Banks' transactions.
- A flock of ravens is called an "unkindness" and can also be known as a "conspiracy".
- NASA adopted countdowns from Fritz Lang's 1929 sci-fi film "Frau im Mond".
- ManhattAnts is a unique ant species found in the cracks of Manhattan pavements.
- The world's oldest wooden wheel, over 5,000 years old, was found in Slovenia.
- Dead skin cells comprise a significant component of household dust, with humans shedding millions of cells each hour.
- Sudan has approximately 255 pyramids, more than Egypt's 138.
- The bumblebee bat, weighing less than a penny, is the world's smallest mammal.

- The human circulatory system extends over 60,000 miles, enough to wrap around the Earth twice.
- Africa spans all four hemispheres and covers nearly 12 million square miles.
- The cornea and cartilage are the only parts of the human body without blood vessels.
- The first animated feature film, "El Apóstol," was made in Argentina in 1917.
- German chocolate cake was invented in Texas and named after Sam German, who created a type of baking chocolate.
- Despite being cast on "The Jeffersons," Marla Gibbs continued working as a flight attendant for two years.
- The Philippines is composed of 7,641 islands, including sandbars and other landforms visible during low tide.
- The Trans-Siberian Railway crosses 3,901 bridges in a single trip and is the longest railroad in the world.
- The Golden Girls' original theme song was supposed to be Bette Midler's "Friends."
- There is sufficient gold inside the Earth to cover the planet's surface with 1.5 feet of gold.
- Cleveland ranked as the fifth-largest U.S. city in 1920, behind Detroit, Philadelphia, Chicago, and New York City.
- Only 0.007% of Earth's water is accessible and fit for human use.
- Wally Amos is renowned for more than cookies; he also discovered and signed Simon & Garfunkel.
- The brand name Spam combines "spice" and "ham" and is not an acronym.
- Water takes 90 days to travel the length of the Mississippi River, which spans 2,340 miles.
- 19th-century individuals consumed arsenic products like Dr. James P. Campbell's Safe Arsenic Complexion Wafers for better skin.

- Annie Moore, a 15-year-old girl from Ireland, was the first person processed at Ellis Island on January 1, 1892.
- Due to thermal expansion, the Eiffel Tower can grow 15 cm taller during the summer.
- Botanically, bananas are classified as berries, whereas strawberries are not.
- A bolt of lightning has enough energy to toast 100,000 slices of bread.
- Honey never spoils; jars found in ancient Egyptian tombs are still edible after more than 3,000 years.
- A day on Venus lasts longer than a year because its rotation period exceeds its orbital period.
- The shortest commercial flight lasts just 57 seconds, connecting two Scottish islands.
- Charles Osborne holds the record for the longest hiccuping spree, lasting 68 years.
- Fred Baur, the inventor of the Pringles can, was buried in one after his death.
- The original oranges were green and originated in Southeast Asia.
- A cow-bison hybrid is known as a "beefalo," bred for its meat.
- Scotland has 421 words for "snow," including terms like "sneesl" (to start raining or snowing) and "feefle" (to swirl).
- Samsung uses a butt-shaped robot to test phone durability.
- Walter Morrison's ashes, the inventor of the frisbee, were made into a frisbee.
- The longest wedding veil extended over 63 football fields, measuring 23,000 feet.
- Scotland's national animal, the unicorn, symbolises purity and grace.
- Bees sometimes sting other bees to protect their hive.

- The first computer virus, called the "Creeper," was created as a joke and displayed the message "I'm the creeper, catch me if you can!"
- Percy Spencer, who discovered microwave cooking, received only \$2 for his invention of the microwave appliance.
- The singular form of spaghetti is "spaghetto."
- The longest gap between the births of twins is 87 days, prompted by their premature birth.
- A baby puffin is known as a "puffling" and is an adorable bird.

Interesting Phobias

- Arachibutyrophobia: Fear of peanut butter sticking to the roof of your mouth.
- Nomophobia: Fear of being without your mobile phone.
- Arithmophobia: Fear of numbers.
- Plutophobia: Fear of money or wealth.
- Xanthophobia: Fear of the color yellow.
- Ablutophobia: Fear of bathing or washing.
- Octophobia: Fear of the number eight.
- Optophobia: Fear of opening one's eyes.

- Globophobia: Fear of balloons.
- Hippopotomonstrosesquippedaliophobia: Fear of long words.
- Ephebiphobia: Fear of adolescents or teenagers.
- Omphalophobia: Fear of belly buttons.
- Linonophobia: Fear of string.
- Pogonophobia: Fear of beards.
- Chaetophobia: Fear of hair.
- Siderophobia: Fear of stars.
- Logophobia: Fear of words.
- Eleutherophobia: Fear of freedom.
- Geliophobia: Fear of laughter.
- Somniphobia: Fear of sleep.
- Alliumphobia: Fear of garlic.
- Phobophobia: Fear of having a phobia.
- Dextrophobia: Fear of having objects to your right.
- Levophobia: Fear of things to the left side of the body.
- Symmetrophobia: Fear of symmetry.
- Asymmetriphobia: Fear of asymmetrical things.
- Kathisophobia: Fear of sitting down.
- Aurophobia: Fear of gold.
- Nostophobia: Fear of returning home.
- Caligynephobia: Fear of beautiful women.
- Kinemortophobia: Fear of zombies.
- Neophobia: Fear of new things and experiences.
- Kakorrhaphiophobia: Fear of failure.
- Aulophobia: Fear of flutes.
- Pediophobia: Fear of dolls.
- Coulrophobia: Fear of clowns.
- Trypophobia: Fear of holes or patterns of holes.
- Hylophobia: Fear of trees.
- Eisoptrophobia: Fear of mirrors.
- Chronophobia: Fear of time passing.

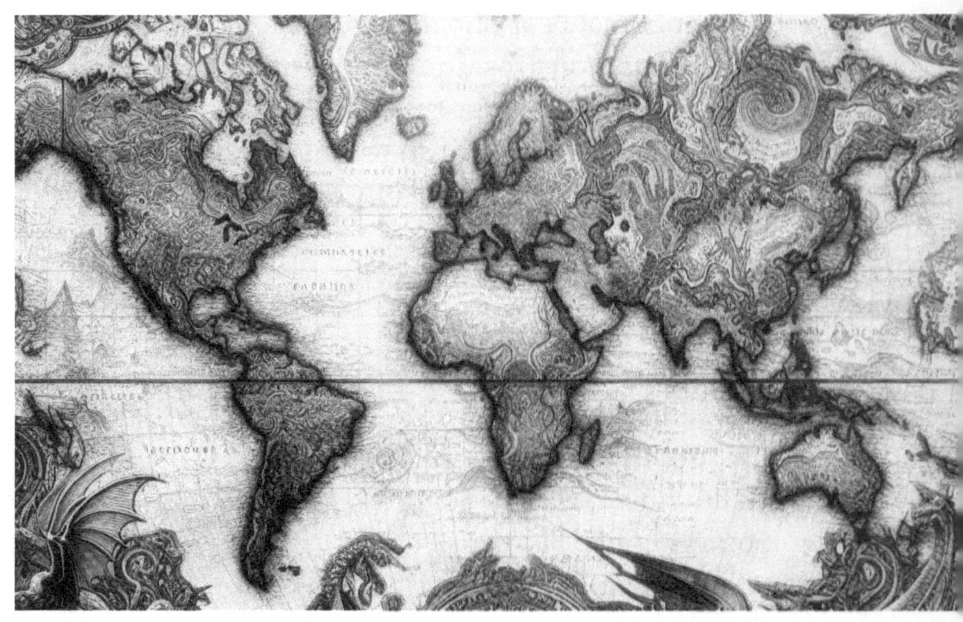

World Geography

- Pacific Ocean: The Pacific Ocean diminishes by approximately an inch each year due to tectonic plate activity.

- Sea Without Coasts: The Sargasso Sea in the Atlantic Ocean is defined solely by ocean currents, lacking any land borders.

- Alaska's Extremes: Due to the Aleutian Islands crossing the 180° meridian, Alaska holds the distinction of being the westernmost, easternmost, and northernmost state in the U.S.

- Largest Desert: Antarctica outranks the Sahara as the largest desert in the world.

- Diomede Islands: Although only 2.4 miles apart, the Diomede Islands in the Bering Strait are separated by a time difference of 20 hours thanks to the International Date Line.

- No Mosquitoes: Iceland stands out as one of the few places globally that is free of mosquitoes.

- Sudan's Pyramids: With over 200 pyramids in Nubia, Sudan surpasses Egypt in the number of these ancient structures.
- Single Resident: Monowi, Nebraska, uniquely has a single resident who also serves as its mayor.
- Languages in Papua New Guinea: Papua New Guinea has the most linguistic diversity worldwide with over 840 languages spoken.
- Tallest Waterfall: Tugela Falls in South Africa exceeds Angel Falls in Venezuela as the tallest waterfall on Earth.
- Floating Islands: Lake Titicaca in Peru features floating islands made from reeds, inhabited by the Uros people.
- Point Nemo: Located in the South Pacific Ocean, Point Nemo is the most remote spot on Earth, farthest from any other landmass.
- Yellowstone Supervolcano: Yellowstone National Park rests atop a supervolcano capable of extensive destruction were it to erupt.
- Oldest City: Jericho, situated in the West Bank, is considered the world's oldest continuously inhabited city.
- Unique Zip Codes: New York City boasts 42 buildings that have their own dedicated zip codes.
- Coldest Temperature: The lowest temperature ever recorded on Earth was −128.6°F (−89.2°C) in Antarctica.
- Lake Within an Island: A peculiar feature in the Philippines includes a lake within an island located in a lake, which itself is on an island.
- Longest Flight: The longest commercial flight covers roughly 19 hours from Singapore to New York.
- Sunniest Place: Yuma, Arizona, enjoys the title of the sunniest place on Earth, experiencing over 4,000 hours of sunshine annually.
- Brazil's Biodiversity: Brazil is exceptionally biodiverse, home to more than 3,100 animal species.

- Mauna Kea: Measured from its base on the ocean floor, Mauna Kea in Hawaii stands taller than Mount Everest.
- Australia's Size: Australia's width surpasses that of the moon by about 600 km.
- Snowiest City: Aomori in Japan experiences over 312 inches of snowfall each year.
- Largest Island: Greenland ranks as the world's biggest island that is not classified as a continent.
- Deepest Lake: Lake Baikal in Russia is renowned for being both the deepest and oldest freshwater lake in the world.
- Longest River: Africa's Nile River is the longest river on the planet.
- Smallest Country: Vatican City is the smallest country globally in terms of both area and population.
- Most Populated City: Tokyo, Japan, is the city with the highest population worldwide.
- Highest Capital: La Paz, Bolivia, sits at around 3,650 meters (11,975 feet) above sea level, making it the highest capital city in the world.
- Largest Archipelago: Indonesia, comprising over 17,000 islands, is the largest archipelago on the globe.
- Longest Coastline: Canada boasts the longest coastline of any nation.
- Largest Lake: The Caspian Sea is the biggest enclosed inland body of water on Earth.
- Most Volcanoes: Indonesia leads the world in active volcanoes.
- Highest Waterfall: Venezuela's Angel Falls is the highest uninterrupted waterfall globally.
- Largest Coral Reef: The Great Barrier Reef in Australia is the largest coral reef system in existence.
- Most Lakes: Canada claims the highest number of lakes among all countries, with over 879,000.

- Longest Mountain Range: The Andes in South America is the longest continental mountain range in the world.
- Largest Rainforest: The Amazon Rainforest stands as the largest tropical rainforest on Earth.
- Highest Peak: At its summit, Mount Everest, part of the Himalayas, is the tallest peak above sea level.
- Largest Desert: The Sahara Desert is the largest hot desert in the world.
- Most Islands: Sweden has the greatest number of islands of any country, counting over 267,570.
- Deepest Ocean: The Mariana Trench, located in the Pacific Ocean, is the deepest oceanic trench in the world.
- Largest Peninsula: The Arabian Peninsula is the world's largest peninsula.
- Most Time Zones: Including its overseas territories, France spans the most time zones of any country.
- Largest Delta: The Ganges-Brahmaputra Delta, found in India and Bangladesh, is the largest delta globally.
- Most Forested Country: Suriname is the leading forested country, with forests covering about 98% of its land.
- Largest Volcano: Mauna Loa in Hawaii holds the record for being the largest volcano by volume and area covered.
- Most Languages: Papua New Guinea is noted for having the most languages spoken of any country, exceeding 840.
- Longest River in Asia: China's Yangtze River is the longest river across Asia.
- Largest Salt Flat: Bolivia's Salar de Uyuni is the largest salt flat in the world.

Strange Collective nouns

- A murder of crows
- A parliament of owls
- A shrewdness of apes
- A cauldron of bats
- A sloth of bears
- A cackle of hyenas
- A bloat of hippopotamuses
- A leap of leopards
- A richness of martens
- A prickle of porcupines
- A crash of rhinoceroses
- A tower of giraffes
- A conspiracy of lemurs
- A romp of otters
- A business of ferrets
- A skulk of foxes
- A murmuration of starlings
- A charm of finches
- A pandemonium of parrots
- A parliament of rooks
- A deceit of lapwings
- A sedge of herons
- A wake of buzzards
- A raft of ducks
- A convocation of eagles
- A bloom of jellyfish
- A quiver of cobras
- A maelstrom of salamanders
- A shiver of sharks
- An intrusion of cockroaches

Grammar Curiosities

- Shortest Sentence: "I am" is the shortest complete sentence in English.
- Pangram: A sentence that contains every letter of the alphabet is called a pangram. Example: "The quick brown fox jumps over the lazy dog".
- Longest Word: The longest word in English is "pneumonoultramicroscopicsilicovolcanoconiosis," a type of lung disease.
- Ghost Words: Some words in the dictionary, like "dord," appeared due to printing errors and have no meaning.

- Common Words: The most commonly used word in English is "I".
- New Words: A new word is added to the dictionary every two hours.
- Crutch Words: Words like "actually," "honestly," and "basically" are often used unnecessarily in sentences.
- Ambigrams: Words like "swims" look the same when turned upside down.
- Language of the Air: All pilots must communicate in English while flying.
- Gender-Neutral: The word "girl" used to mean a young person of either gender.
- Contronyms: Words like "bound" can mean both "tied to a place" and "heading to a place".
- Silent Letters: About 60% of English words contain silent letters.
- Rhymeless Words: Words like "month" and "silver" have no perfect rhymes in English.
- Synonyms and Antonyms: English has a rich vocabulary with many synonyms and antonyms.
- Contronyms: Words that have opposite meanings in different contexts, like "cleave" (to split apart or to adhere closely).
- Palindrome: A word or phrase that reads the same backward as forward, like "madam".
- Anagram: A word or phrase formed by rearranging the letters of another, like "listen" and "silent".
- Homophones: Words that sound the same but have different meanings, like "to," "too," and "two".
- Homographs: Words that are spelled the same but have different meanings, like "lead" (to guide) and "lead" (a metal).
- Portmanteau: A word blending the sounds and combining the meanings of two others, like "brunch" (breakfast + lunch).

- Acronyms: Words formed from the initial letters of other words, like "NASA" (National Aeronautics and Space Administration).
- Initialisms: Similar to acronyms but pronounced as individual letters, like "FBI" (Federal Bureau of Investigation).
- Eponyms: Words derived from the names of people, like "sandwich" (named after the Earl of Sandwich).
- Toponyms: Words derived from place names, like "champagne" (from the Champagne region of France).
- Loanwords: Words borrowed from other languages, like "ballet" (French) and "piano" (Italian).
- Neologisms: Newly coined words or expressions, like "selfie".
- Backronyms: Acronyms formed from an existing word, like "POSH" (Port Out, Starboard Home).
- Tautonyms: Scientific names where the genus and species are the same, like "Gorilla gorilla".
- Capitonyms: Words that change meaning when capitalized, like "Polish" (from Poland) and "polish" (to make shiny).
- Mondegreens: Misheard song lyrics or phrases, like "Excuse me while I kiss this guy" (instead of "kiss the sky").
- Eggcorns: Misheard phrases that still make sense, like "for all intensive purposes" instead of "for all intents and purposes".
- Malapropisms: The mistaken use of a word in place of a similar-sounding one, often with unintentionally amusing effect, like "dance a flamingo" instead of "flamenco".
- Spoonerisms: The swapping of the initial sounds of two words, like "tease my ears" instead of "ease my tears".
- Oxymorons: Phrases that combine contradictory terms, like "jumbo shrimp".

- Hyperbole: Exaggerated statements not meant to be taken literally, like "I'm so hungry I could eat a horse".
- Litotes: Understatements that use double negatives, like "not bad" to mean "good".
- Euphemisms: Mild or indirect words substituted for ones considered too harsh, like "passed away" instead of "died".
- Dysphemisms: Harsh or blunt terms used instead of more polite ones, like "croaked" instead of "died".
- Metaphors: Figures of speech where a word is applied to an object or action to which it is not literally applicable, like "time is a thief".
- Similes: Comparisons using "like" or "as," like "as brave as a lion".
- Idioms: Phrases with meanings not deducible from the individual words, like "kick the bucket".
- Proverbs: Short, commonly known expressions that offer advice, like "a stitch in time saves nine".
- Clichés: Overused phrases that have lost their original impact, like "think outside the box".
- Palindromic Sentences: Sentences that read the same backward and forward, like "A man, a plan, a canal, Panama!".
- Heteronyms: Words that are spelled the same but have different pronunciations and meanings, like "lead" (to guide) and "lead" (a metal).
- Polysemy: Words with multiple meanings, like "bank" (financial institution or the side of a river).
- Antanaclasis: The repetition of a word in two different senses, like "If you aren't fired with enthusiasm, you will be fired with enthusiasm".
- Anaphora: The repetition of a word or phrase at the beginning of successive clauses, like "I have a dream".

- Epistrophe: The repetition of a word at the end of successive clauses, like "See no evil, hear no evil, speak no evil".
- Chiasmus: A rhetorical device in which two or more clauses are balanced against each other by the reversal of their structures, like "Never let a fool kiss you or a kiss fool you".
- Tmesis: The separation of parts of a compound word by an intervening word or words, like "abso-bloody-lutely".
- Paraprosdokian: A figure of speech in which the latter part of a sentence or phrase is surprising or unexpected, like "I've had a perfectly wonderful evening, but this wasn't it".
- Syllogism: A form of reasoning in which a conclusion is drawn from two given or assumed propositions, like "All men are mortal. Socrates is a man. Therefore, Socrates is mortal".
- Zeugma: A figure of speech in which a word applies to multiple parts of the sentence, like "He stole my heart and my wallet".
- Synecdoche: A figure of speech in which a part is made to represent the whole, like "all hands on deck".
- Metonymy: A figure of speech in which a thing is referred to by the name of something closely associated with it, like "the White House" for the U.S. president.
- Epanalepsis: The repetition of the initial part of a clause or sentence at the end of that same clause or sentence, like "The king is dead, long live the king".
- Anadiplosis: The repetition of the last word of a preceding clause at the beginning of the next one, like "Fear leads to anger. Anger leads to hate. Hate leads to suffering".
- Polyptoton: The repetition of a word in a different case or inflection in the same sentence, like "Who shall watch the watchmen?".

Notes